KAZU

AND

THE RAINBOW BRIDGE

THIS BOOK BELONGS TO

_____

FOR THE KIDS WHO WANT TO EXPLORE

ISBN: 9798894582863

KAZU WAS A CURIOUS TABBY CAT WITH SOFT, STRIPED FUR. ONE RAINY AFTERNOON, A MAGICAL RAINBOW APPEARED IN THE SKY, SHIMMERING WITH BRIGHT, GLOWING COLORS.

KAZU BLINKED IN SURPRISE. THE RAINBOW SEEMED TO TOUCH THE GROUND RIGHT BY HIS GARDEN. "I'VE NEVER SEEN THAT BEFORE," HE THOUGHT, STEPPING CLOSER WITH WONDER.

SUDDENLY, THE RAINBOW SPARKLED, AND A GOLDEN BRIDGE APPEARED. A GENTLE VOICE WHISPERED, "CROSS THE RAINBOW BRIDGE, KAZU. A MAGICAL LAND NEEDS YOUR HELP."

KAZU PLACED ONE PAW ON THE GLOWING BRIDGE. WITH EACH STEP, THE WORLD AROUND HIM SHIFTED INTO A SWIRLING, COLORFUL MIST OF RED, BLUE, AND YELLOW.

WHEN THE MIST CLEARED, KAZU STOOD IN A STRANGE LAND. THE GRASS WAS BLUE, THE SKY WAS PINK, AND THE AIR HUMMED WITH SOFT, MUSICAL NOTES.

"WELCOME, KAZU!" SAID A PARROT WITH SHIMMERING FEATHERS.
"THIS IS COLORLAND. OUR COLOR OF KINDNESS HAS VANISHED.
WITHOUT IT, PEOPLE ARE BECOMING GRUMPY."

KAZU TILTED HIS HEAD. "HOW CAN I HELP?" HE ASKED. THE PARROT FLAPPED ITS WINGS AND SAID, "FOLLOW THE GLOWING FOOTPRINTS TO THE CRYSTAL CAVE."

KAZU SPOTTED THE GLOWING FOOTPRINTS. THEY SHONE SOFTLY, LIKE GOLDEN STARLIGHT, LEADING TOWARD DISTANT, SPARKLING MOUNTAINS. HE TOOK A DEEP BREATH AND FOLLOWED.

THE PATH WOUND THROUGH FORESTS OF SILVER TREES AND RIVERS OF
RAINBOW WATER. THE FOOTPRINTS GLOWED BRIGHTER AS KAZU WALKED
CAREFULLY THROUGH COLORLAND.

IN THE DISTANCE, KAZU SAW THE CRYSTAL CAVE. ITS
ENTRANCE SHIMMERED WITH SWIRLING PATTERNS OF LIGHT.
"I MUST FIND KINDNESS HERE," KAZU WHISPERED.

INSIDE, THE CAVE WAS COLD AND QUIET. IN THE CENTER STOOD A CRACKED CRYSTAL HEART, DULL AND GRAY. "THE HEART OF KINDNESS!" GASPED KAZU.

"WHO DARES ENTER?" BOOMED A VOICE. A SHADOWY FIGURE
APPEARED: GRIZZLE, THE COLOR THIEF. "KINDNESS MAKES
PEOPLE STRONG. I TOOK IT AWAY!"

KAZU STOOD TALL. "KINDNESS BRINGS US TOGETHER! WE NEED IT BACK!" GRIZZLE LAUGHED AND SENT DARK SWIRLS TOWARD KAZU. "YOU CAN'T STOP ME!" HE SNEERED.

KAZU REMEMBERED HIS FRIENDS AT HOME, SHARING WARMTH AND KINDNESS. "KINDNESS IS STRONGER THAN FEAR!" HE SHOUTED. HIS HEART GLOWED, AND SOFT, GOLDEN LIGHT BURST FORTH.

THE GOLDEN LIGHT WRAPPED AROUND THE CRYSTAL HEART. THE CRACKS DISAPPEARED, AND THE HEART BEGAN TO GLOW BRIGHTLY WITH A SOFT, COMFORTING WARMTH.

"NO!" CRIED GRIZZLE AS THE GOLDEN LIGHT SURROUNDED HIM.
HE SHRANK SMALLER AND SMALLER UNTIL HE DISAPPEARED INTO A TINY, GRAY SPECK.

THE CAVE FILLED WITH RAINBOW LIGHT. THE HEART OF KINDNESS PULSED GENTLY.
"THANK YOU, KAZU," SAID THE VOICE OF THE CAVE. "KINDNESS HAS RETURNED."

KAZU STEPPED OUTSIDE. THE SKY WAS NOW A WARM, GOLDEN COLOR.
FLOWERS BLOOMED WITH BRIGHT COLORS, AND THE AIR BUZZED WITH HAPPY LAUGHTER.

THE PARROT FLUTTERED DOWN. "YOU DID IT! COLORLAND IS FULL OF KINDNESS AGAIN."
KAZU PURRED PROUDLY. "KINDNESS MAKES EVERYTHING BETTER," HE SAID.

THE RAINBOW BRIDGE APPEARED AGAIN. "TIME TO GO HOME," SAID THE PARROT.
KAZU WAVED GOODBYE AND STEPPED ONTO THE GLOWING PATH.

KAZU CROSSED THE BRIDGE, THE MAGICAL MIST SWIRLING AROUND HIM. WHEN IT CLEARED, HE STOOD BACK IN HIS FAMILIAR GARDEN.

THE RAINBOW FADED INTO THE SKY, BUT A GOLDEN GLOW LINGERED IN KAZU'S HEART. HE SMILED, KNOWING HE HAD MADE A DIFFERENCE.

THE NEXT DAY, KAZU SAW HIS NEIGHBORS HELPING EACH OTHER AND SMILING MORE. THE MAGIC OF KINDNESS HAD SPREAD INTO THE REAL WORLD, TOO.

KAZU STRETCHED IN THE SUN. "KINDNESS IS THE BEST KIND OF MAGIC," HE PURRED, AS A TINY RAINBOW GLIMMERED ABOVE HIM.

www.ingramcontent.com/pod-product-compliance
Lightning Source LLC
LaVergne TN
LVHW081703050326
832903LV00026B/1875